I0755987

FINISHING LINE PRESS
www.finishinglinepress.com

Between Sunsets

Poems and Vignettes by

Yvette J. Green

Finishing Line Press
Georgetown, Kentucky

Between Sunsets

ISBN 979-8-89990-425-7 First Edition

ACKNOWLEDGMENTS

Immense thanks to these journals for publishing my original poetry:

Hive Avenue, "For My Choices"
Isacoustic, "Yarn"
Indolent Books: What Rough Beast, "A Single Cardinal"
Silk + Smoke, "In Memoriam (For K.M.)"
The Mark Literary Review, "The day has chosen to rest"

Publisher: Leah Huete de Maines
Editor: Christen Kincaid
Cover Art: Yvette J. Green
Author Photo: Wade Thomas
Cover Design: Elizabeth Maines McCleavy

Order online: www.finishinglinepress.com
also available on amazon.com

Author inquiries and mail orders:
Finishing Line Press
PO Box 1626
Georgetown, Kentucky 40324
USA

Contents

How to Write a Poem: Listen

Incline your ear to the poem it will tell you what to do
let it breathe
sense what desires to find itself on the page

Listen to what is in the atmosphere waiting on you
Do not let doubt get in the way
of the poem's release

the words,
the backstory will propel you forward
Let the poem glide you across the page

Use the music of your memories to
Ground yourself on the land:
do not resist the truth

The ancestors will speak to you

after you have finished gathering
and are ready to rest
the poem whispers to you

For My Choices

For weeping on my wedding day

and choosing not to walk away
from what I did not want,

I owe my younger self
Crisp white orchids on spindly spines
offering me beauty in triplicates—
not the orange Asiatic lilies
with which I walked down a cement aisle
near a man-made lake towards
a man who did not love me.

For failing to taste my own tears

and choosing to be wedged
between wisdom and weakness,
when I asked everyone,
but myself if I could walk away
while
8 months with child.

For all the bad choices that gave me abundance,

I owe myself
a purple sky that hosts sunsets
singing of love
and spring dreams whispering lyrics
of who I am.

Yarn

Impossible to navigate the narrative you spin
Yarn unfolds
from the mint green skein your mother used
to knit our son's baby blanket
and from the berry ball her calico cat batted
around the kitchen tile

The yarn has rolled under the sofa
out of your reach.

I rewrap the tendrils
tightly to contain the spun thread
to crochet another memory, for another day.

I place the wound strands in
stoneware clay
and stow them in the curio cabinet
where I keep my dolls.

Red Poinsettias in March

How do I tell my plants
their season has ended,
that their leaves should have turned
green
or shed completely,
that 3 months later,
their time has come?

How do I discard
what no longer fits
into this new season
Of cherry blossoms,
green sprouts,
and lemon tulips?

What do you do with that which refuses to bend
to the will of what should be?

To the Lady in the Purple Skirt at the Grocery Store

Seafood met me as the automatic doors yielded to my presence. Even though fresh fish was in a department at the back of the building, the grocery store's ventilation system was struggling to exhale fresh air. Thus, it poured scents of shrimp and salmon on visitors immediately as they entered the store. An odiferous welcome on every occasion.

I was in the midst of a divorce and running in to grab a few items for dinner before picking up my children from their after school care and daycare. I recounted how busy I was, ever irritated, bemoaning my lot in life and a never ending chore list.

You were a grandmother. A purple skirt dropped from your waist and experience adorned your face.

"I cannot get my shoe back on." You said as you steadied one hand on your cart and attempted to slide your foot back into your flat. You had created a makeshift shoe horn from folded paper. I could not understand how your choice of assistance would be successful, yet I was hopeful. I tried to provide an anchor. A friendly smile. Good vibes. I was hopeful that being a cheerleader offering encouragement from the sidelines would be a catalyst for you to help yourself.

All were insufficient.

"Can you help me?"

Your foot, too, had stories baked into them, causing cracking and dryness. Though I tended to carry curiosity and a desire to bear witness with me, I knew in this instance I didn't need stories from your feet, and there must be another way to be helpful and of service. I was slowly registering that since I was the only one near in the midst of your struggle, I was going to have to make a choice.

I thought about my hands making contact with your foot. About touching your shoe. About inhaling a smell that rivaled what the grocery store's HVAC system coughed up.

I thought about what your daughter and granddaughter would have wanted for you, because I thought about what I would have wanted for my grandmother. I knew I was called for such a moment as this, yet I wasn't ready.

I took a deep breath and bent to the floor, picked up your shoe, and ushered in your foot. I pulled the heel of the shoe so that it would grab your ankle and ensured the fit was snug.

Relief found you. You smiled and thanked me.

In a matter of seconds, I was back on my feet and we were no longer conspicuously couched between apples and roses at the front of the grocery store.

"Whatever you did for the least of these, you have done for me," I recalled from Bible study.

Not that you were the least of anyone. But rather your need, this act, forced me to confront the edges of comfort. To choose something unpleasant. To sacrifice my self-involvement in order to help you complete your shopping.

Your need widened me. Opened me up to giving when it wasn't easy. My hands had been tightly wrapped around my circumstances and my lack. I sought to control as much as I could, stressing myself and my children in the process. I was scared and sad and selfish.

This wasn't a random act of kindness I had chosen. It wasn't paying for the person's meal in the drive-thru behind me when I had extra money. This wasn't tutoring kids as a volunteer, nor was it buying extra toys at Christmas to give to children without. This was an opportunity for humility and compassion, a chance for me to be aware of your feelings and to refrain from turning up my nose and scrunching up my face as I touched your foot.

Did I run to the restroom after the exchange to double wash my hands? Or did I apply globs of hand sanitizer to my palms and fingers? Did I only pick up wrapped items and leave fresh produce for another day: a day when my hands had not directly touched someone else's bare foot?

Did I make you a grandmother in my head, based on how I classified the elderly? Did you feel exposed or embarrassed? Did you grow concerned about aging gracefully and losing easy navigation through the world? Did you share this moment with your daughter or granddaughter, hoping to teach them compassion? Or had years in this world taught you that asking for help was not a weakness? That aging gracefully was a foolish, trite adage? Were you aware that certain requests and needs give others an opportunity to show up disrobed of their ego and self-involvement? Did you know of the gift you gave me by baring yourself?

In Memoriam

(for K.M.)

(They said antioxidants were weapons.
Prayer, positive thinking,
community, and antioxidants.)

She showed me her battle scars:
how they cut off her left breast,
described where the port was positioned,
how she fit the prosthesis into her bra,
her belief in the prophet,
who said she would be healed.

She was majestic,
a warrior
with knotted roots:
her husband left,
but still expected her to show up
at their church as his wife,
and she did.

A solid trunk:
she stood beside me
when my husband left,
shouldering some of my burden
as her own bones began to deteriorate.
With branches
that reached to the heavens:
Before I went to the courthouse,
she had me praise God for his favor.

Her crown began to slip:
When I had bronchitis,
the cells multiplied,
invaded her lungs.

Between sips of green tea and a return to the earth,
She prepared me for war.

Gluttony

I grip tightly
the pain—
and cradle the slap
that still scalds my tawny cheek—

I nourish the blame, the abandonment,
the ash—
and gnaw at the flesh of my palm through
an unmanicured fist
as I walk into
this new relationship.

new love

he kisses my latent pain
and rubs it back to life

chooses fingernails
to unearth my scabs

and unveil unhealed lacerations

he calls this love

softness

I didn't know I was soft
until he was in awe of
how my arms felt against
his calluses

When I'm alone with
my own form
I'm leftover dough from
homemade biscuits
raw, yeast, scraps

But when I'm with him,
I'm supple, Italian leather
vegetable tanned by time,
under his lamp
I warm
and his rugged edges,
acute tongue
full of tungsten
slacken slowly, relax
in the folds of my love.

When Sunsets Come Too Soon

(For Shamika)

She was my girlhood.

Shamika and I were eight months apart to the day, born in the middle. Holding hands. There were four boys born before us and five boys born after us, a mix of our own brothers and cousins. She was my only girl cousin for ten years.

She was always happy to see me whenever summers and weddings returned me to New Orleans to visit my matrilineal family. No specific moments marked my time with her in any monumental way.

I'm sure we went to the Audubon Zoo. Ate crawfish in our uncle's backyard. Walked to a neighbor's house to get huckabucks. And drank pineapple Big Shots while mosquitos feasted on our thighs.

Though she was the one with whom I played "Apple on a stick, makes me sick, makes my heart go two, forty-six," Shamika was a presence more than anything. A joy. An energy. Light and laughter. My girl cousin.

We shared secrets, all of which have since vanished, and a shared sense of place in our family. We'd hug when I arrived in New Orleans and again when I left, returning home to Nashville.

As our teen years turned over, I chose to go to school in my family's city, but by then my girl cousin was no longer in the Big Easy. She had moved to the Pacific Northwest. Miles and miles meant losing touch.

When our grandfather turned eighty, we both returned to New Orleans for the big celebration. We hugged tightly, held our babies, and caught up on the fifteen years or so that we had missed in each other's lives. She had recently turned thirty-three; I would join her in seven months. We were draped in the light of Mardi Gras and familial love. We hugged as we said goodbye and promised, this time, to stay in touch.

But we didn't.

And then our grandfather died.

Seven years had stretched distance further.

On the morning of his funeral service, our family gathered for the procession into the church. I entered the gathering space, hugged, and kissed family members in the upper room of the church.

I made my rounds, smiling, until I saw her.

A veil was rent.

I fell into her arms and wept.

She held me.

We slipped backwards in time, neither adorned in too grown for our age, nor dispossessed of our youth.

Memories had been stitched deep inside of us. Buried beneath baby fat and divorces and withstanding moves to different coasts. Flyover states had taken us away from each other.

Our youth joined us at forty years old as we stood in our familial line to enter the church together. She tucked my arm beneath hers and we walked down the center aisle of our grandfather's home church St. John Divine Missionary Baptist. We sat behind our parents, aunts, and uncles, soaking tissues side by side.

Our second cousin, Nadra, sang a hymn to send our grandfather off. When Nadra recognized the gift her voice provided, she kept filling up the church, even as the pastor stood up to signal "Give me that microphone." She sang another verse, another refrain, signaling to the pastor, "Sir, sit down. I'm here for my family, not for your funeral service timeline."

During the repast, we laughed at the pastor who, unable to persuade our cousin to stop singing, was forced to resign and return to his seat. All of our cousins spent the evening together drinking and laughing, remembering and hoping for more times of communal joy without the sting of grief bringing us together.

Laughter and sunshine and a special girlhood because we had each other.

Social media kept us in touch as much as it was able.

Then, almost six years after we buried our grandfather, Shamika had a foot injury.

An orthopedic boot encapsulated her foot and leg. Micro-tears had attacked my own Achilles heel a few years earlier.

We both mothered fiercely, but did not always take the best care of ourselves.

Something about cardiac arrest.

"What did you say? Can you explain that again?" I asked her brother when he called with updates. His explanation still did not bring me clarity.

A blood clot. Had traveled.

I waited for more updates, some sense-making tools. I went to work and walked through my day heavy, weighted, more tired than usual.

Unresponsive.

Text messages flew. Information was passed through phone calls. From my uncle/her father to my mother/her aunt.

Life support.

I refused to let anyone outside of my family in. Public tears would be kept at bay.

Prayers. Hope for miracles and healing.

Our girlhood, encoded in my body beyond memories of jumping rope, broke loose again.

Words lacked power to explain the overwhelm, how off-kilter I felt at what was ahead despite our friendship being so far away from us.

I spotted grieving after it had begun. It insisted I recognize what was happening in my body. To put a name to this thing I could not grasp.

We waited.

Barrettes and plaits and hand games were bowing out.

Her eldest son would make the final decision.

Something about lack of oxygen to her brain for too long.

It was time for my cousin to rest.

Only 46, with children beneath her wings. She had been a wonder.

My girlhood was growing smaller.
A piece of me was leaving.
Life is but a vapor.
My heart would ever-ache.

How to Write a Poem: Sense

It is in the pluck of a hair
from your chin
and the clink of the tweezers
when you lie them on the counter

It is in the air that enters your nostrils
when you inhale for 1-2-3-4 counts
and the air you let go of
through your mouth for 1-2-3-4 counts

It's in the hum of the HVAC
the pulse of the silence
the echo of a baby crying
when the child is all grown up
the s t r e t c h i n g of your skin
acrosssssssss longgggggggg dayssssssss
at home

In the breath you gather to blow out a candle that
breathes calm into your space
the folding of the laptop in a barely there click
the clack of the microwave door closing behind you
the pop of elastic as your panties struggle to hug your growing
ass
the crunch of bone on bone
when you kneel as cartilage dissipates
and the glide between crisp sheets not weighted with dead skin
the poem climbs out of the score of being home

new love II

when the sun is cheeky, and she
stretches slowly
yawns widely
laughs at squirrels throwing acorns at passersby
plays hide and seek with the clouds
winks as you take out the trash
kisses your forehead
and loves you fiercely:
know all is right with the world

For you

Will you take the moon if I give it to you?
It isn't a yellow daisy or a peace lily,
nor is it a suicide pact thwarted
by the morning sun.
It won't heal writer's block, nor will it transcribe
the interviews for your dissertation.
It won't atone for the hatred that engulfs us,
nor will it help your son make wise decisions.
It won't remedy all that is wrong with the business
of education.
But if I give you the moon,
will it diminish some of the moodiness in your
9 p.m. sky?
Will it remind you of the poems you've written?
Will it touch that absence in your being?

I've made my decision.
I give you the Crust Moon
because the season for
melting and
refreezing
has ended.

Intertwined

Wrought iron love
between me and my sisters
who were not my sisters,
chases us
towards an end goal
we can not see.
We interlace our fingers,
jump from the 3rd platform and
land like felines
in the middle of our childhood dreams.
Backwards we rush,
blindly searching through marbled memories
that explain a barely-there beginning.
Beneath concrete, we crouch,
ready to pounce on interlopers
who seek to untangle our braided bond.
We push away each other's nightmares.
And set ablaze
the somber shadows
that keep us from
ascension.

When Sunsets Come Too Soon

(For L.C.)

In the middle of spring, an old friend went on to find peace. We taught in the same school, in the same department. We had children within the same age range. I babysat her son and daughter a few times and watched them grow up through pictures, stories, their visits to the school, and Facebook. As she had done with mine.

We had shared students. Ones we cared about and those we admonished. Those who failed to complete assignments or learn from our too-late grammar lessons. Students who said we were their favorite teachers. Those who frustrated the hell out of us. And those whose smiles made the day better. We shared losses. And wins. Graduations. Return visits. And relief when a school year ended.

We commiserated about the poor decisions our administration made. And about the challenges of teaching in a specific high school, in a specific school district.

Wedding showers for colleagues. Sadnesses. Joys. We sent colleagues who were charting new territories on their way with goodbyes and good lucks. She did the same for me when I separated from the school after ten years.

There was a period where four of us had homemade sangria in the park listening to live jazz by the water. On the Potomac. Or sangrias at the bar in a favorite restaurant with tapas on top of tapas.

Both of the other women from our former quad called me within minutes of each other to share news I couldn't take.

She was only 41.

A basketball pummeled my chest. My body took a hit even though I hadn't seen or spoken with her in a few years. I crumpled.

I ached for her children. Young people losing their mother is an injustice beyond quantifying and naming. Maybe I can shoulder some of their pain, so they will hurt just a half-centimeter less. Just enough so they can rest and weep, release and hold tightly, grow around their grief that will never leave, and move forward.

I share the loss with my two friends. We reminisce and hold a knowing of what sharing people for extended periods of time does to the body, even as silent years race by.

The weight of carrying pails of water together never fades. Hands from separate bodies toting one glorious burden. Tears forming as we spilled the pails' contents and again when she told a story that made our stomachs hurt from laughter.

Building our castles.

Telling the truth and shaming the devil.

Biting our tongues.

Eating bread and drinking wine.

Together.

For Us, or Dancing Poetry

We will dance:
this act is
poetry.
when we
weep,
we choose
to be
strong
and this
strength is
poetry.
We will hold
each other's burdens;
to share sorrow
is poetry.
Poetry
is sorrow;
each other's burdens
we share.
Poetry
is.
to be strong
is what we choose.
when we weep lines of poetry
this act is a dance.

A Cardinal

A fierce cardinal
on a stone-gray day
amongst trees that await spring
on a tattered fence.

He shows up

Unaware,
or maybe very aware
that I need him.

He reminds me there is a season for everything
and today is the season to stare at him

To follow his wings as he ascends to the highest branch
To wait for him to return before me

He never returns my gaze
He doesn't break the fourth wall
Though he knows I'm there
He understands my need to participate from behind glass

He shows me how to be mindful
He sings a praise song

This is the season to need
a single cardinal
in a single frame

untitled

Peace is not believing, in giving up hope. A release of all
the unworthiness they told me to feel. Tally them.
They had no problem with my decision to settle.

All the ones I've known weren't generous enough to know
me. They tried to make me into someone else. They were in
love with what they chose to see. Shortsighted. I acquiesced.

But water pushes and pushes until it makes a
way out, or through.

They failed.

They tried again. They returned after an unexcused absence.
They offered: recommittals, expensive earrings, and promises
not to lie again.

Water is formidable. Stronger than piss poor,
man made levees.

All the ones I've known lacked space. There was no room for the
me they couldn't see.

I am of water. Flowing. Dynamic. Viscous even,
ever-moving beneath the story they saw.
Growing thicker and broader. Too thick to fit
into the small space they offered.

Too powerful to believe the story of
unworthiness they told me.

How to Write a Poem: Choreograph

Move in free verse
with your hips
wide, full, feminine.
Part your lips to mark time—
the hips carry the narratives
listen to
the feminine
the moment has to be held
and carefully passed down and passed on.

Hold something of home in your hips,
the feminine
will reveal exactly what to
remember

—the accumulated sounds of communal memory
rest in the body

Immerse yourself in the language of the dance
listen to the sequence

Orchestrate your movements
with the score
that you write
from your hips

Learn the counts 2-3-4.
Watch how the feminine moves
the accent is in your pelvis
the rhythm is in their dialogue
the beat tells the story.

Do not edit yourself
Embrace the feminine
follow your hips in order to
Choreograph the poem

Garden Duplex

(after Jericho Brown)

I force myself to stare at my faults
I grant space for noxious weeds to seed

Weeds in my garden are obnoxious to me
They win with shrewd remarks in thought bubbles I can see

I lose when they see my thought bubbles.
They create measuring sticks with raised eyebrows

Raised eyebrows reveal how I lose; they measure me.
Sages prosper in poor soil, in native hatred

Native hatred haunts the dreams of the sage
I touch a four leaf clover to become enough

Four leaf clovers aren't in my garden
I baptize me in the light of myself

I baptize myself in the love for myself
I force myself to recognize the fault lines are underground

For Today

May we feel the sun love our faces.
to help us focus on joys, old and new.

May autumn's jewels bring us moments of stillness
so we get lost in their beauty.

May water flow and offer waves
that calm our sympathetic nervous systems.

May a good book show us ourselves.
And a chai latte warm our hands.

May we release unnecessary hindrances
and grip tightly to gratitude.

May we choose wisely
that which brings us peace and lifts us up.

May light be ever near
and when it's not,
let us be the light.

Like the Bees

I want to be divine like the bees.

They float from white clover to white clover.

Those little flowers I used to pluck from the soil and tie
the stem around itself. Offer a chant, "Mama had a baby and
its head popped off," and pull the stem to make the blossom
jump to the ground.

My friends and I selected the longest ones. Tied the end of
one stem to the head of the next flower until we formed
a bangle that fits eight-year-old wrists.

It is only in mid-life that I gape at a bee bowing the longer
stemmed flowers. I am enamored with the bee sensing which
blossoms are no longer laden with pollen and then flit on its way.

The bounce in his flight lacks the weight of worry. A
determination to connect with each flower, to gather
what is needed, to fill up, exceed, overflow, to consume the
perfect amount. To take and to give.

I want to be born for a task such as this. A divine order
guiding my trajectory. I want to inspire growth and drip
honey like Basquiat's paint. To be light and attuned, using all
of my senses to fulfill a destiny.

The Day Has Chosen to Rest

The sun met me
as the moment was dying.
We shared stories
of love and loss,
peace and chaos.
She wrapped herself
in lilac and orange quilts
and went to sleep in my soul.

Yvette J. Green lives Prince George's County, Maryland. Her two sons awe, bless, and inspire her. She is an educator with over twenty years' experience at both the high school and college levels. Yvette's writing explores culture, travel, family, inheritances, and mental health. Transitions and nature often demand her attention and call her to the page. An essayist, memoirist, and poet, Yvette experiments with form and at times, weaves verse into her creative nonfiction.

Yvette is a graduate of Xavier University of Louisiana (BA) and University of Maryland (MA). She is an alum of Tin House's Winter Workshop. Yvette's poetry can be found in *45th Parallel, The Mark Literary Review, Silk + Smoke, Backwards Trajectory,* among others.

Her creative nonfiction has been featured in *Salon, Slate, Viator, midnight & indigo, MUTHA Magazine, Brevity Blog* and anthologies *Seasons of Our Lives-Winter: Stories from WomensMemoirs.com and Mamas, Martyrs, and Jezebels: Myths, Legends, and Other Lies You've Been Told about Black Women. Between Sunsets* is Yvette's debut chapbook.

www.ingramcontent.com/pod-product-compliance
Lightning Source LLC
LaVergne TN
LVHW090540110826
845146LV00003B/1203

* 9 7 9 8 8 9 9 9 0 4 2 5 7 *